"I have been a fan of Jim Zoller's poetry for over twenty-five years and have been eagerly awaiting the publication of Living on the Flood Plain. Whether Zoller's poems focus on nature, particularly the river, or on his family life, they are always life affirming, though not naively so. Zoller realizes that we must have hope while living in an 'age easily bored, hungry to laugh but seldom happy,' but he also understands that life is messy. People get divorced and die just as a river brings both life and destruction."

PETER JOHNSON, winner of the 2001 James Laughlin Award

"In these deeply elemental poems, Jim Zoller finds in the clay and silt of the Genesee River the strata of the human heart. Alongside the current of his patient voice, we compost our 'darkening stories' so that we might grow into the light. This collection begins on the flood plain and finally emerges—dripping, gritty and worshipful—on the near edge of higher ground."

PAUL J. WILLIS, author of Bright Shoots of Everlastingness

"In this carefully structured collection, Zoller presents several tightly woven sequences of interlocking poems. Many of these pieces are attuned to the turning of seasons—the river's rise and fall, freeze and thaw. Such closely observed depictions of nature reflect the poet's spiritual sensibilities in a way that seems reminiscent of Thoreau. While often introspective, they move seamlessly between the personal and the universal: reading the landscape for traces of the past, what could be simply erased if the river should rise, reckoning what is at stake with the loss of a parent, spouse, or child. The landscape he finds harbors memories that remind us of our deepest bonds to one another—'remind us just who we are'—and the emotions that ultimately mean most. We reenter our lives at moments overwhelmed by what we have learned to recognize as mercy: 'how/ God so casually and deliberately, with such prodigious and exacting care,/ graces the homely, the feeble, the disrepaired.' These meditations on landscape and loss ultimately offer a form of redemption as 'All become[s] testimony…[to] our letting go.'"

CHRISTIAN KNOELLER, winner of the 2007 Midwestern Heritage Prize and author of Completing the Circle

"In these poems Jim Zoller bring us close to the land, close to the turn of the seasons, and, yes, to dark days of storm. But the words seek not flash and filigree, but come measured and intelligent, bringing us into the presence of a knowing observer. The voice is patient and considering—the wise voice of father and husband and teacher. These poems do what all good poems should do—take us to a place on earth and make it live, make it matter."

MARK DEFOE, author of *The Rock and the Pebble*

LIVING ON THE FLOOD PLAIN

LIVING ON THE FLOOD PLAIN

James A. Zoller

30 March 2009

For Laura

Who begins a life
Sweetly afflicted with words.

Enjoy, fellow writer

[signature]

WordFarm
LA PORTE, INDIANA

WordFarm
2010 Michigan Avenue
La Porte, IN 46350
www.wordfarm.net
info@wordfarm.net

Copyright © 2008 by James A. Zoller

All rights reserved. No part of this publication may be reproduced, stored in a retrieval system or transmitted in any form or by any means, electronic, mechanical, photocopying, recording or otherwise, without the prior permission of WordFarm.

Cover Image: iStockPhoto
Cover Design: Andrew Craft
USA ISBN-13: 978-1-60226-002-3
USA ISBN-10: 1-60226-002-8

Printed in the United States of America
First Edition: 2008

Library of Congress Cataloging-in-Publication Data

Data applied for.

P 10 9 8 7 6 5 4 3 2 1
Y 14 13 12 11 10 09 08

*for Donna, my life companion,
and for our small ones, who have
grown into friends*

CONTENTS

GALLERY ONE: *Watercolors & Charcoals*

WATERCOLORS
- The Flood Plain 15
- When Rain Begins 16
- What I Say, What Water Says 17
- Standing Water 18
- Beyond the Crest 19
- The Good Earth 20
- The Life of the River 21

CHARCOALS
- New Snow 25
- One Must Survive 26
- Breaking the Ice 28
- What the Stream Says 29
- The Interval 30
- Romance of Air and Bones 31

GALLERY TWO: *Landscapes*

CANEADEA SILT STUDIES
- Caneadea Silt 37
- An Abandonment 39
- Alone in an Irregular Field 40

THE FLOOD SEQUENCE
- The Flood 43

LATTICE BRIDGE SEQUENCE

Bone Memory 59
Soundless Water 61
Forgotten Bridge 62
What Winter Graces 63

GALLERY THREE: *The Permanent Collection*

This Most Obvious of Things 67
Bottle 69
My First Husband 71
Saying Goodbye 73
Elegy for Many Voices 75
Words for his Widow 77
Currency 80
Pilgrim 81
The Classroom 82
The Old Fears 84

Gallery Notes 86

GALLERY ONE:
Watercolors & Charcoals

*Already too much has happened
that was not supposed to happen,*

———————

*Whoever wanted to enjoy the world
faces an impossible task.*

*Stupidity is not funny.
Wisdom is not cheerful.*

———————

*there are no questions more urgent
than the naive ones.*

Wisława Szymborska, "The Turn of the Century"

Watercolors

THE FLOOD PLAIN

The old hills, the ruined tree-covered hills,
gouged and littered and rounded by the last ice age,

eroded and furrowed by rain and runoff,
shift little by little, crumble, drift toward the valley.

It will take centuries and more as it has taken centuries.
The river snakes its way slowly north

following the ancient trail of ice,
the river-bank graveled and flat,

the water broad and shallow, undercutting banks
and taking, in its seasonal torrent, trees

and tall grasses along the overhang, rocks and boulders
released and rolled, gravity borne and water borne

into its wide shallow bed, its untidy trail,
the valley wide and green, a vast river-fed flood plain.

WHEN RAIN BEGINS

Leaves of the sycamore, broad
as grape leaves, hang
dull and listless.

Hill pastures burn
brown along the valley
stretching north and south,
where the river, sluggish
and tepid, wanders
through the dry gravel
of its bed.

The sun bakes the stones, heats
pavement beneath my feet,
lays fiery hands upon my head
and shoulders.

Before rain comes
it burdens the air—
dry air embracing rain
before it finds ground.

Then begins that steady drumming,
solid now in the air,
finding ground,
a hard wind
welcomed in a withering land
that drives weak
and strong alike
to shelter.

WHAT I SAY, WHAT WATER SAYS

When I shout from the hillside vivid with goldenrod
    from unmowed fields, yellow and brown

when I shout toward the river, distant and hidden,
    wandering through sheltering trees

my voice returns, echoing deep in the valley
    my words rise like water from low ground

my voice like a child lost to his visions
    full of sorrow I'd thought buried or drowned

Each hill, as I climb, gives rise to another
    a journey to gain higher ground

each day, I am drawn as shadows turn eastward
    like a rivulet snaking its way toward the river

When I shout from the hillside sodden with rainfall
    from unmowed fields, burdened and bowed

when I empty my voice into rain busied silence
    the river rises and washes it back

the sound of the water is a sound first soothing
    then a fluster, like geese taking flight

 the voices of water are peace
    and despair

STANDING WATER

Where water lies on low ground, grass dies.
Its smooth surface, that mirrored sky, slowly clouds.
Water striders haunt its face, mosquito larvae
hang mysteriously below the blue reflection,
a mud-turned-dirt ring trails its slow recession.
Where water finds rest, decay begins.

Who is to say the life that attends its dying—
frogs, mosquitoes, water bugs, algae, mud life—
is *less* necessary, *less* worthy, *less* living?

Are we to say *one but not the other?*
—the falling, streaming, soaking, filling but not
the wandering, eroding, this hanging around?

And do we not judge, as it drives us away,
that earthy, once welcoming air turned stink?

BEYOND THE CREST

We wait for the terrible heat to rise
bearing its blanket of damp air,
beneath a sky that remains grey,
that never lifts, that never turns blue.

I have risen early to work but cannot;
channels through which thought must pass
remain as blurred by haze as the distant hills.
The strong light carries heat but no shadows.

Overnight the river below the house crested
and began to fall, its filthy sludge
clinging still, like wreckage, to the trunks
of shore trees, branches, roots, flaming foliage.

It will clear soon. In a matter of days, perhaps,
the air too will clear, the mind to follow.

THE GOOD EARTH

The slow sun lingers, lazy beyond the tree-lined river.
Morning lies like dew on my skin, morning

honeyed with ripening corn and the sour drift
of dung, clumped where I stand amidst green stalks.

Though no wind stirs, corn leaves rustle,
layered on the complex rhythms of locust and crickets.

In the long river valley between Paradise and Bliss,
I walk in a good place, on earth vivid and rich.

My senses are full. It is not a matter of choice.
God is good. I am as true a believer as any.

Yet as I skirt the stone marking and closing the old road,
stand on the broken deck of the doomed bridge,

regard the river, I see myself in the dark current.
God help me, the weight I bear. I, most blessed of men.

THE LIFE OF THE RIVER

One would not begin with glaciers.

Begin with moving water,
    at lake-fed streams and springs.

Begin at headwaters, then—this gathering place
    for snowmelt or ground water
    finding its way through rock and sand.

The lake, we say, is spring-fed or snow-fed,
    emits a stream at its lower end—
    and this, too, this stream knows gravity.

When snow melts, dry hills run.

In spring, dry stream beds fill,
    rush madly as rapids, leap

from any high stone in its eagerness
    to become river, to bring life,
    to carry earth on its back.

This is what we say: We say *this river
    has life*; we say *this river is life*; or
    we say *this river is like life—it is more
    than itself*. When life ends, the river goes on.

So, the headwaters, a beginning, cold,
    a present holding past and future.
    And it means—for us—everything.

Charcoals

NEW SNOW

It has begun to snow again,
dime-sized white flakes filling the air
    as if they were swirling in the dense water
        of a snow globe.

The plow scrapes past with its circling amber light
and its blade that curls the snow back on itself
    like revolving seasons.

I sit at my table by the window
at the threshold of a new century
    expecting to write about myself and my times
        expecting somehow a rush of ideas and voices.

Finally, the body I choose is the body I live in.
Taking whatever tools I have—paints, gestures, words
    table knife or scalpel—
        I begin to cut.

Now the snow has tapered off,
the temperature drops. No one is on the street,
    no sounds sift through the air.

This might be the end of time,
    the end of the world.

But something tells me—reason, habit, memory,
faith—that life must continue, that I
    have a tool somewhere to stanch the bleeding.

ONE MUST SURVIVE

I am acquainted with the labors of poets in an age that sets poets below clowns—in an age easily bored, hungry to laugh but seldom happy.

Each morning—my mind yet uncluttered—I go to my table and find an empty page in my notebook.

Each page is white like snow outside my window, though it bears no marks from deer who come during the night, who graze on the myrtle or nibble, as high as they might reach, the soft needles of the yew.

From the warm distance of my window, I examine these tracks. This is how one begins these labors. Fix the tracks in the mind. Fill the tracks with language, make a mold.

Following tracks is not the same as watching deer whose night travels are nearly silent and whose hungers drive them near our houses while even dogs sleep.

Neither myrtle nor yew make a sound. No sound the page. Only the slow hum of the furnace blowing clouds from its vent.

This winter world of dark and deep cold and continuous snow is a hard world. Behind walls and windows we close our eyes against it, make our bodies small.

It is humbling, being neither farmer nor priest. I have little to show for my morning. The early sun has left my window, its shadows shifted, softened.

I set down my pen, examine my notebook.

Across the page tracks of thought litter the white surface. Something has been pawing all right, finding just here the soft, nourishing needles.

I know the ground. I know the cold. I know hunger.

I know work.

BREAKING THE ICE

gathering strength in its
downward rush the stream

flexes beneath ice
that has held since December

breaks it free of its anchors lifts
and slides the huge plates from its path

pushes before it the walls
of its winter prison

as mad, brown water surges
over and around its banks

looking for a shorter path
through fields through quiet streets

clamoring to rejoin the rampage
falling into cellars shouting as it runs

once in that bedlam at the point
I could no longer hear myself think

—as if it were called
by the voice of God—

I heard my name

WHAT THE STREAM SAYS

This morning I hold the cold iron rail
and lean over the dark roiling water to listen;

fog brought by warm air over thawing ground blots
even the lowest limbs of the trees.

Upstream, the spring-fed stream rushes from fog
and vanishes into fog on the far side of the bridge.

The sun tarries. It is dark. I listen.
The voice of this water carries the voice of all waters.

It is legion, it is multitude, it is choral,
it draws the ear as fire draws the eye.

It is life force, it is destruction. I listen,
listen for the sound of drops, of one drop,

the soft plosive *plop plop plop*
from a leaf as snow melts,

the sound of each falling calling its truer self,
calling as if *indifferent* life depended on its voice.

THE INTERVAL

when snow is gone from streets
and from ground beyond

—snow banks reveal their gritty selves
grow black and hard
with sand and silt

the interval between snow
and excess of daffodils
is the interval
we crave and dread

the ugliness of life
hidden in winter
overwhelmed by spring
follows us—waiting

just here, just now
—to remind us just who we are

ROMANCE OF AIR AND BONES

Along the dead-end street
you and I walk hand in hand,

listening to the soft snow
drifting through this gray afternoon,

watching flakes light upon
our dark winter clothes.

When you speak,
dark-limbed trees lean in,

the sky brightens.
When you speak, your words

appear in the cold air,
land upon my ears and lashes,

white grows transparent
—your day my day float,

dance in air weightless as snow,
lightened by love and talk

—those ephemeral white crystals,
commonplace of true companions.

GALLERY TWO:
Landscapes

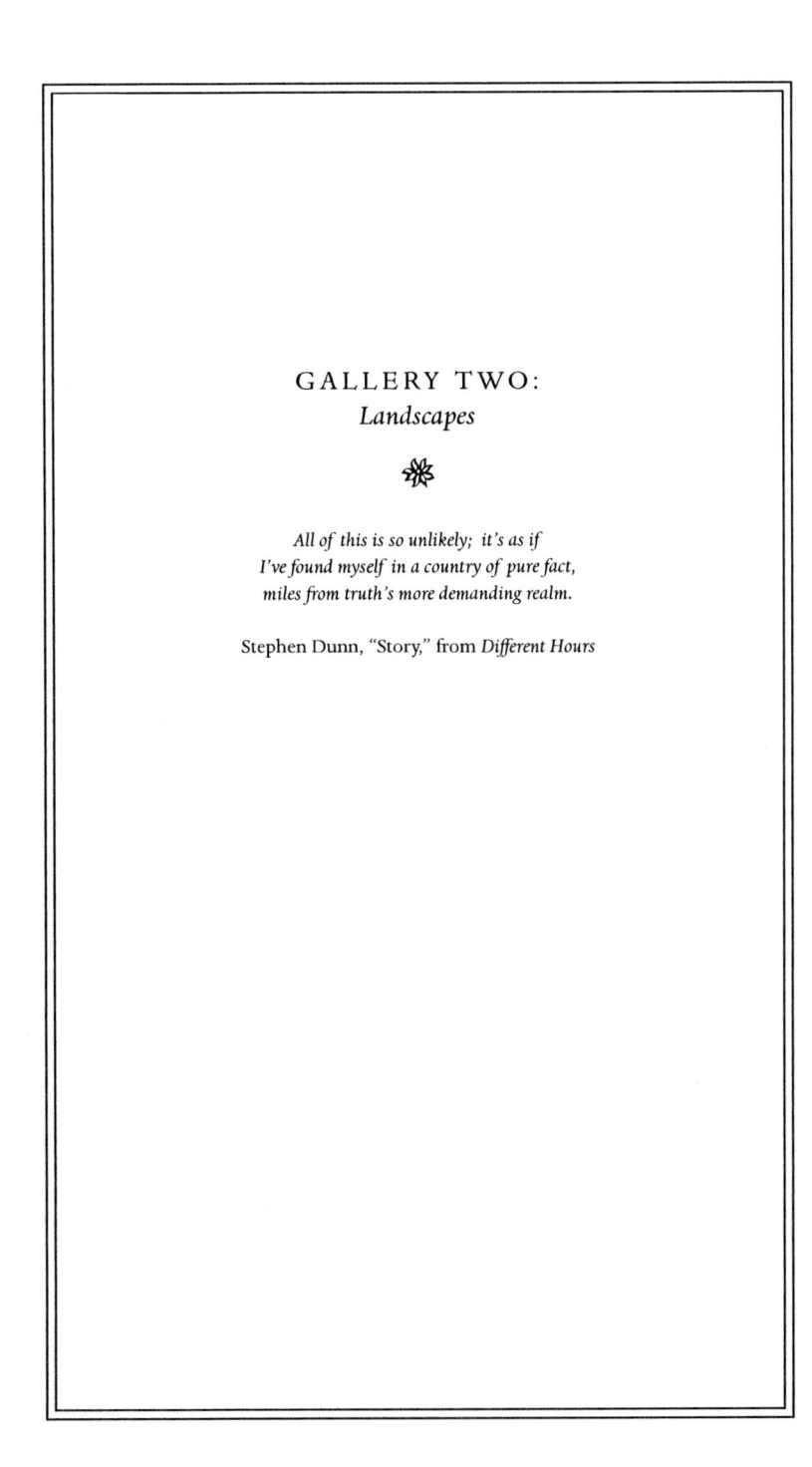

❊

*All of this is so unlikely; it's as if
I've found myself in a country of pure fact,
miles from truth's more demanding realm.*

Stephen Dunn, "Story," from *Different Hours*

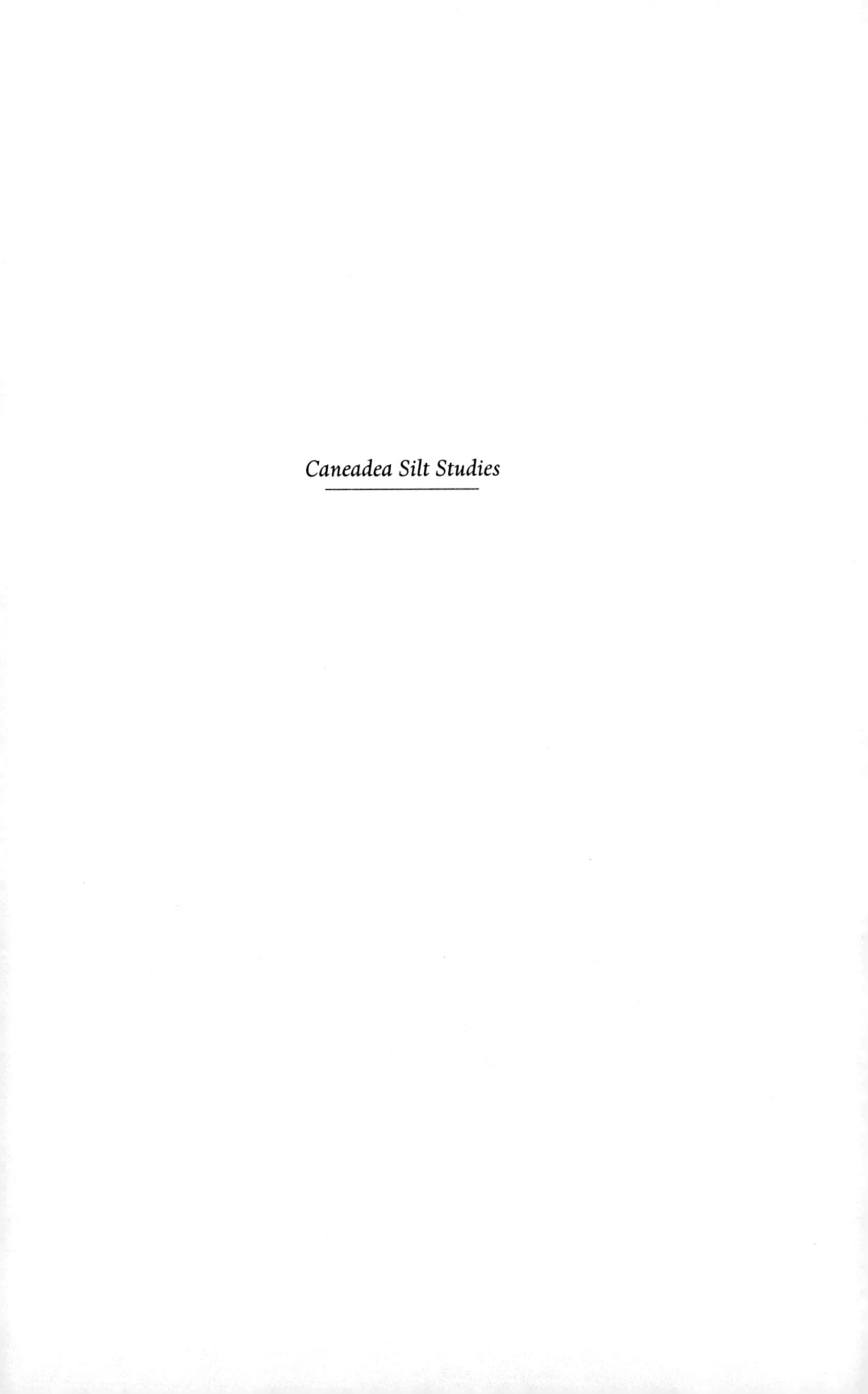

Caneadea Silt Studies

CANEADEA SILT

In these clay hills where water lingers
where rain makes pools in fields where
streams run grey from clay-wash in spring,
the land tends to sheer, hillsides breaking, sliding.

Not on Claybed Road but on Tucker Hill—
where pavement approaches the ravine
the road settles every so often, dropping
two inches this year, six the year just past.

And on Centerville, though less violently.
And Seymour, patched to hide fault lines.

The surface of the road, tarred and smooth,
is suddenly indented, as a pine board
struck and marked by an errant hammer.

Like gossip, malicious soft-ground stories
began to circulate, a form of country legend.

A man excavating a slope behind his house
discovered the land would not be dug.
The hole refilled itself. Then the backhoe
had to be hauled out with a tractor.

Caneadea silt, said the county agent, *quicksand,
a gift from the last ice age, like gorges and kettle ponds.*

So we build with an eye toward the river,
fill in the roads as they tear and slide, then live
as though ground beneath us will always hold.

AN ABANDONMENT

When November rains strip the last browned leaves,
and newly spartan trees withdraw
to weather the coming cold, the hard bones of our nakedness
drive us indoors, make us somber, hard to live with.

Along county roads through these hills, along
this river valley, the story of our leavings, our miseries,
tales of wasted opportunities, our appetites,
unfold for any traveler willing to linger.

Failure to manage our many things shows through—
seedlings growing from gutters, moss on the shingles,
scraps of lumber and wall board thrown behind bushes,
the broken toilet growing families of mice—all to be hauled away.

All become testimony. Down the road one neighbor's dead car
marked by weeds, another's porch with chairs oozing cotton,
abandoned sheds, collapsing barns, hay bales sinking into soil.
Marks of our poverty, our labors, our holdings. Our letting go.

ALONE IN AN IRREGULAR FIELD

Alone in a cornfield at a bend in the road,
an irregular clearing, bordered by tall trees.
Deep in that field among its own sheltering
trees, surrounded by once-tended lilac and yew,

sits an empty house, as deep brown and grey
as weathered wood can be—unbroken glass
still visible in its second floor windows,
the bones of its roof still square, walls plumb.

For twenty years, I have wanted to visit that house.
I have wanted to trespass that field through tall corn.

I have wanted to knock at its rough door, to push it open
on its singing hinges and smell its age, its age,
to hear my *hello*s echo through its rooms.

Soon it will be too late. Twenty years more,
should I remain to pass by, the lines that lash it to earth
will break its roof ridge. Glass will shatter.
Winter will enter. Weather that colors leaves along its faces,

the urge that forces corn from seed,
that forces new seed, will crack it open like a shell,
will draw it down slowly but slowly
will compost its darkening stories into soil.

The Flood Sequence

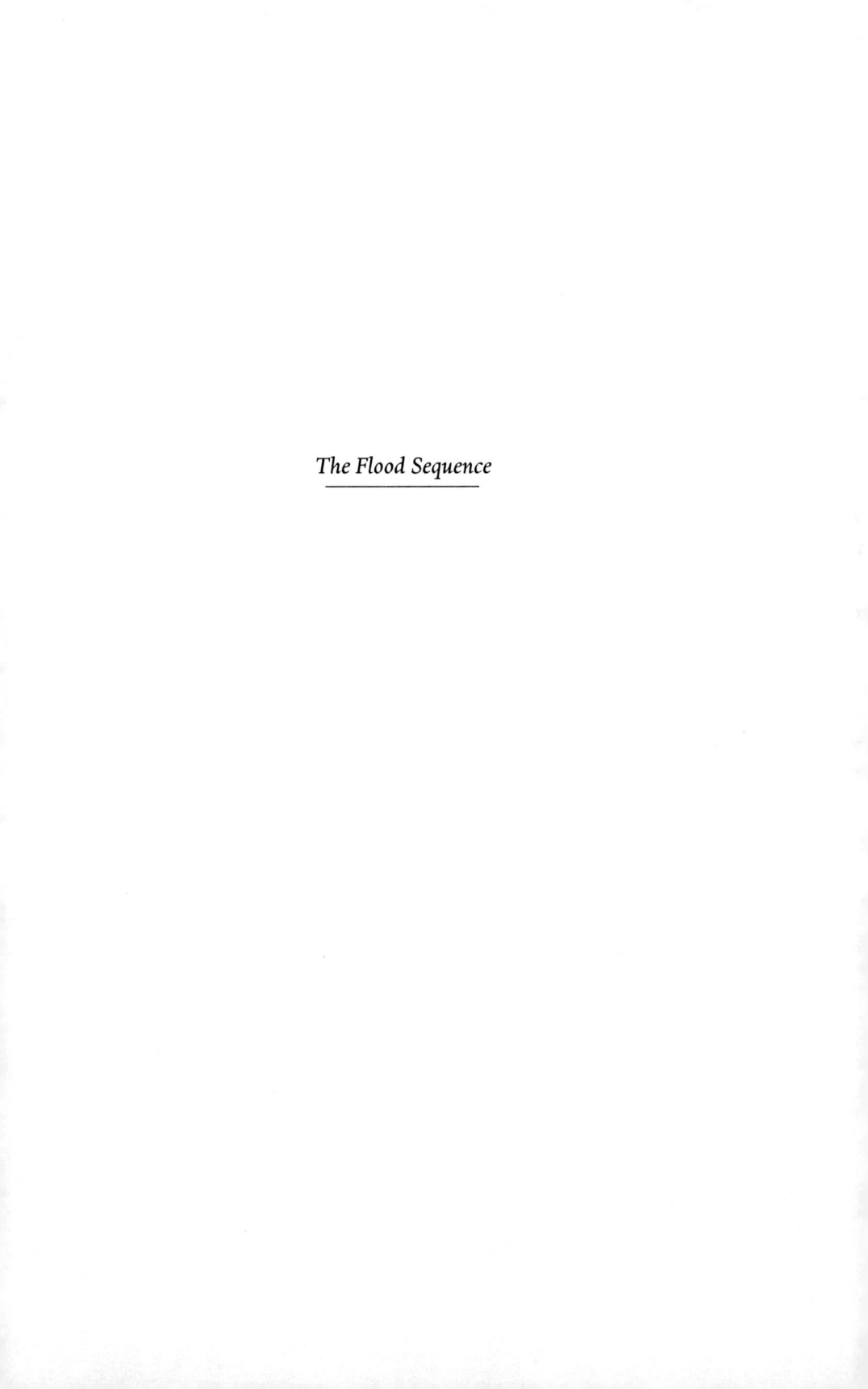

THE FLOOD

I
My view is simple.

The road, the highway north and south, runs beside the river.

Long before humans began fishing its banks, the river had
flattened out its bed, a fact that has made road building easy.

It has made travel easy too,
as the road follows the old forms of water travel
to the towns and villages that spring up along the river,
settlers like seeds carried downstream on currents,
deposited where the river bends.

Or where the water eddies and slows,
where the weightier objects settle out.

II
Four miles north, narrow and dark with rust, the closest bridge
spans the river, hidden by stores at the intersection,

by 19th Century buildings with tall facades, peeling paint, faded
signs—then by houses, by a bend in the road itself before the steel-
deck bridge

and by trees—locust, willow, sumac, American Sycamore, scrub
pine, oak, maple. I have lived here many years, but I know only
common names

and of these only a few.

III
Seven miles south a second bridge
stands six blocks from the highway, hidden by a town common
with trees and flag pole and a stone watering trough.

On a corner across from a concrete-block bar, a 19th Century
house with ginger-bread woodwork, lately used as a bed and
breakfast.

Ragweed haunts its tiny formal garden
where an old farm wagon sags behind the wrought-iron fence,
its place in the soil already orange with iron drippings.

On the next block, behind the commons near the firehouse, stand
three brick churches, side by side. Methodist, Baptist, Catholic.

Then houses again. Trailers set on foundations to look like houses.

Just past the bridge the road, now gravel, winds up into the hills.

IV
Today, the river lies off the map of concern.

It skirts the town. It stays to itself.
It lies beyond the trees, on the other side of the levee.

We cross it when we must, fish when time and mood allow,
swim when we are hot.

We live where we naturally settle.

We are at ease with our lives on the flood plain.
We are at peace with the river.

V
But for the shrubs, bracken, teasle, Queen Anne's lace,
but for thistle, the tall grasses, sumac, trees—but for these,
we might see water as we travel that road.

So we go weeks or months without seeing the river.

It is there all along but out of sight and beyond recall.
We forget the river.

But what does that matter. We are human, after all.
Memory is short.

VI
Not now swept by wind nor weighted by rain
leaves drift silently after the delicate manner of leaves

into the mumbling stream
which seeps still from ground desperate for rain

until cold-hardened rocks narrow the channel
beneath the bridge where your shadow darkens water

its surface pocked by flakes drifting silently
after the delicate manner of snow.

VII
This morning as I write with pencil in my composition book,
the town snow plow scrapes along the street.

I feel it in my feet and through my chair before I hear its rumble.

I see it dimly through the gently falling snow beyond my window.

Then the wind picks up and obliterates everything except
pieces of white air. The yellow truck disappears, though
I hear it, feel it, for some minutes longer.

Later I will test how serious the snow is, how dangerous
the falling temperatures. I will go out to buy a newspaper, to read
about the world beyond, further down the whitened road.

VIII
As is my habit, I cross a footbridge below my house at least twice a
day walking to and from my office. The footbridge spans a stream
that runs from the hillsides and empties into the river perhaps a
mile down its serpentine path.

For several years the stream has been frozen and snow covered in
January.

This year a gash of open water ten yards long and eighteen inches
wide cuts through the snowfield just above the bridge, allowing
deer to come and drink, allowing me to follow their sharp tracks.

Grey water moves rapidly in this protected spot in the ravine,
among the trees, out of the wind.

At the top of the ravine at the far side wind blows clouds of loose
snow over the snow embankments, reminding me of photographs
of the Matterhorn. Of Everest.

Wind becomes swift water in the treetops.

IX
After weeks of temperatures circling zero
the frozen branches of maple and oak
clack together in the wind,

their groans in hard gusts like the groans of ice far out on the lake.

The sound of branches sliding against one another
is the sound of an old door.

It is the sound of a stricken animal,

the sound of distress from a sleeping child.

It will stop you in your tracks.

It says *listen*.

Listen.

X
In late winter as snow begins to recede from road and path,
from west and south facing hillsides, the river grows,
fills its wide, rocky bed.

When the water rises overnight, we say it has "come up."

During spring rains, too, the river rises, and after thunderstorms in summer.

When the water comes up, it dislodges old tree limbs that have fallen into its banks or wedged between rocks.

Sometimes a current lately come up will undercut the bank and uproot trees and carry these along like leaves. Eventually, these trees, whole living trees, are tossed up and scattered along the bank down river

—or, as the water recedes, they are dropped in the riverbed itself.

Sometimes leaves on these uprooted, rootless trees will stay green all summer as if life wishes to continue, to go on, to follow its natural course.

XI
We live on the flood plain, we watch the river rise and fall,

we hear its voice change from whispers in the dry season
   to profound vibrations of diesel locomotive in spring.

We know its seasons and its impulses. Still, inexplicably, no one
   expects floods.

We live here.
It has been so many years. We take it for granted. We forget it.

We take no precautions.

This is natural. We are foolish.

We trust.

XII
How your catastrophe might have come upon you
so suddenly, so powerfully, so destructively
as to sweep you away and fill us with grief

how we missed and misread the signs

how we all hoped and trusted and went about our business

cannot be explained in what we salvage.

Ruin stains everything like soiled water.

XIII
What does one expect?

Does water resist gravity?

What should we demand of each other?

Can we live without trust—in constant fear and vigilance?

Have we been careless? Or unreasonable? Or foolish?

Or stupid?

XIV
I am not a bad person, she said.

Or did I imagine she said what she said

as I imagine in the cool, rain-damped world
that spring will never turn hot and dry?

XV
What is a bad person? I say.
An apple turns bad in a thousand ways.

Sometimes it rots from the inside
without showing outward signs.

   Why not people?

If I drown someone, does that make me a killer?
Is dying always a bad thing?

   Am I bad because I let someone drown?

XVI
Long after the spring waters recede a line of thunderstorms thrash
across our hills. For hours it rains as it might in the tropics.

Water runs down the street like a river.

From a narrow ribbon, the stream below my house explodes
into an angry torrent. At the approach of summer solstice the
afternoon grows dark.
Late at night fire sirens sound.

The stream that had been ankle deep at noon is six feet deep and twenty feet wide, roaring through its hairpin corners, hauling debris of any kind—whole trees, brush, bushes, boards, trash—to where the streambed narrows at a footbridge,

where everything holds fast.

Suddenly the water has nowhere to go but over its banks, filling fields and yards and basements, running north and south along the main street of town, spreading wherever it can.

XVII
But it didn't mean anything
To me, it was not significant

I didn't set out to break my vows,
I didn't deliberately break his heart,

I didn't leave him from malice or hatred or rottenness inside.

I have been honest and truthful throughout.
   Doesn't that count for something?

I don't want you to think badly of me. I am
the same person I was.

I am not a bad person.

   A good person then?

Yes.

A good person who did terrible things?

Yes.

For no reason?

No, she said. I did those things for me.

XVIII
The loud water drops its debris at the footbridge, clogging the streambed.

Detoured, water gushes across the grass, impatient to rejoin the river.

It sweeps mud, silt, gravel, odds and ends out of the streambed across lawns and fields, into the streets and basements, down stairwells and window wells, through tiny spaces in door frames and foundations, into the engines and under-carriages of cars.

Rising water reaches the frames of houses and soaks into wood, devouring insulation in outer walls, submerging furnaces and snuffing water heaters, overpowering sump pumps, soaking cardboard boxes, basement furniture—

dropping what it must, shouldering what it might, even houses and cattle, when it has strength. And speed.

And surprise.

XIX
We live on the flood plain.

Your wife has gone suddenly

for no reasons but her own.

Water suddenly out of its banks, turbulent, roiling, ice cold, racing headlong, racing to sweep you away, to fill you with silt, eddying and swirling at your feet, your knees, cutting channels, scoring the landscape, filling in and overrunning,

carrying what it might carry—suddenly dangerous and frightening.

If not now, sometime in your life.

This is the flood, the riverbed breached,
the danger upon us,
the need urgent urgent

panic rising from the cold grip of water around your thighs.

XX
And in that moment,
that split second as your body
begins to scramble against the tugging, rising water,
to grasp at any solid object, to find
any high ground

—at that precise moment your life opens its galleries

every corrosive image,
every regret, every misdirected word and thought
plays itself out
before your mind's eyes
as if time itself had stopped,
as if this were Judgment Day.

Now, you think, how *could* this have happened? What did I do to bring it on?

The only voice you hear roars,
it is angry,
it is many voices,
it is within you,

it wants to sweep you away.

It has swept into your life. It has ruined your business.
It has become your life, your business, your only concern.

We live on the flood plain.

The only voice you hear
is the voice of water.

XXI
the palpable roar,
so dense it makes air itself hard to endure, the deafening urgency
of the currents, the sliding, slippery ground beneath your feet

the sound of your heart, suddenly insistent, the sound of your
breathing, labored, harsh, rasping

the sound of hope being swept away

XXII
As water recedes,

you slog through leavings that in some hard to imagine future
will make the land vivid

wasted ground as promised land.

Smell the river water and mud and muck.

It is the smell of death and decay, of carcasses, whole, new and
rotted, water bloated cattle, goats, of compost swept from hillsides,
from ravines where we dump our refuse, where we dump our
rusting freezers and stoves.

The smell of ruin.

It shall be, one day, your smell and mine.

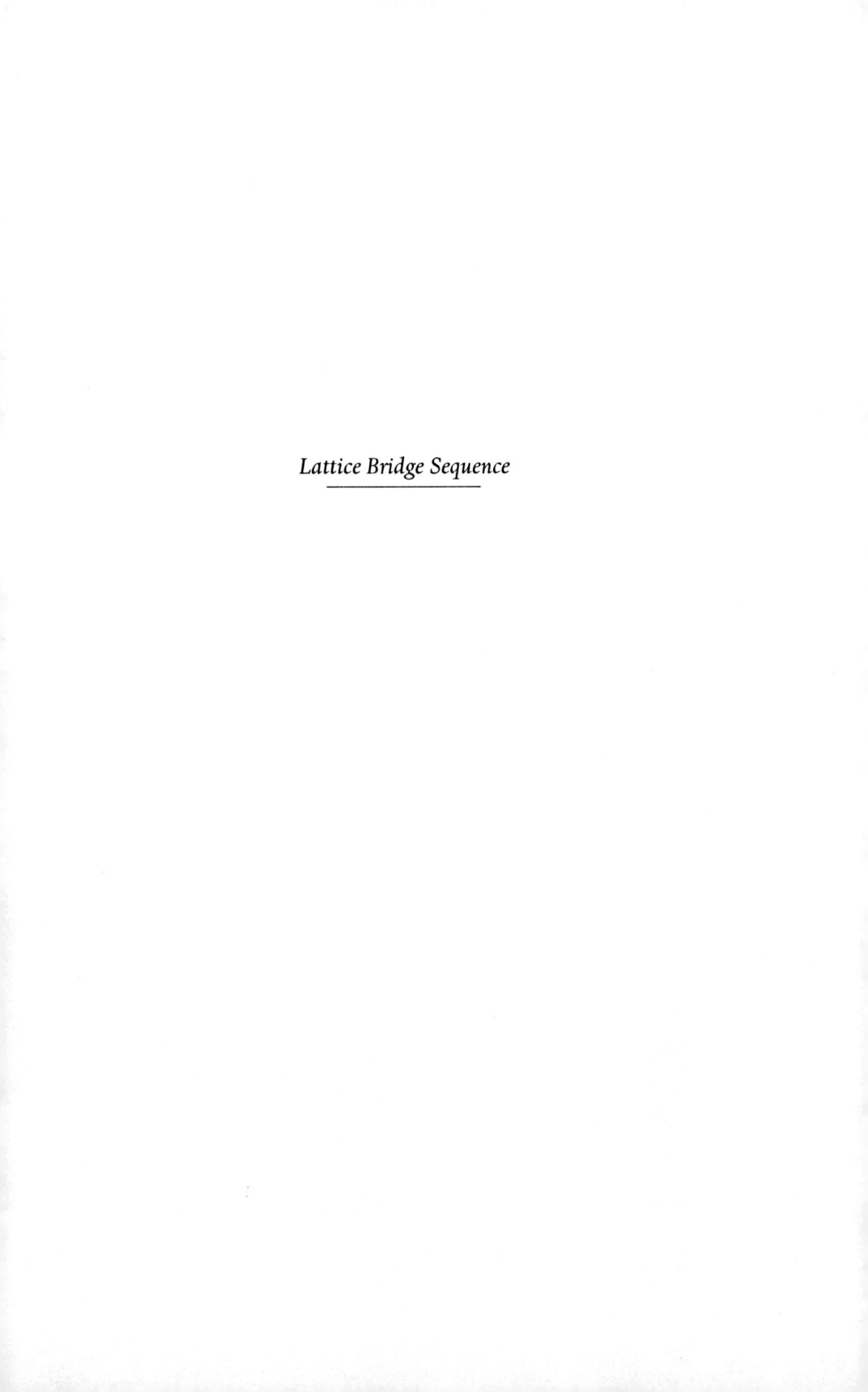

Lattice Bridge Sequence

BONE MEMORY

The rusting green I-beams of the lattice bridge,
neither profound nor elegant, arc
over the high water of the river. Slender steel rods
like threads of a web spun from the high beams
suspend the deck—planks, weathered dark, patched
with plywood, rotting and fallen away here and there.

A guard rail fence defends each approach.
No car has navigated its narrow channel for a generation.
I have come to see it, driven to the end of the dead-end,
and pushed through tall weeds to where it rises before me.

So I straddle and dismount the guard rail as if it were a horse.
To skirt it would mean wading through the tall tangled
grass and briars of the old road embankment. I stand
on the last bit of concrete, my toes touching the damp-dark wood
decking—the cloudy river rushing straight at me,
then miraculously sliding beneath my shoes and reappearing
   beyond.

High and muddy, the river swirls and rushes close
to the ruined deck. The sight of river muscle so near
to my feet sends a shock through my bones the way
unfenced heights send shocks through my legs,
paining my feet and ankles. In another time or place
I might call it fear. Dread. Bone memory.

I look across to the far bank, married to the near bank
by this useless rusting arch. With time enough and the right
   courage,
as, say, the fearlessness of adolescence, one might cross even now,
easily perhaps despite the warnings and treacherous footing.

SOUNDLESS WATER

At my feet the orchard grass and dandelions have taken hold,
ventured onto the bridge deck, rooted in cracks and rotting wood.

Overhead, through a screen of leaves, the deep blue of the spring
morning sky radiates. Perfectly. Water here, today, is so nearly
soundless, I can hear the clap of birch and cottonwood leaves. No
breeze stirs the grasses.

Yet, should I forget myself, the pull underfoot
would sweep me downstream
and bury me without hesitation.

FORGOTTEN BRIDGE

I leave my car in the unplowed snow at the end of Lattice Bridge
Road, cross the guardrail barricade, and venture onto the deck.
Rectangles of plywood have been set over weak spots. A section,
big as the shadow of a pick-up, is simply gone.

Snowy arches rise overhead mirroring the naked limbs of trees
along the shore, each with its own sleeve of snow, its manacles of
ice—each tree defying the toppling sheer of winter wind, dignified
in its ordinary struggles, graced by new snow.

Early sun that slants through the trees, lighting up the snowy
lattice, does not touch the water.

Because I cannot search the face of God, I come here to search His
voice. I am not the first. The prints of birds and foraging animals
track the decking like small complaints. Who is to say what we
seek? Who is to say what advantage the bridge will lend?

Without having ever imagined your grief, I find myself overcome.
For this, too, no language suffices.

But here: the voices of dark water, soothing, unintelligible,
and the voices of light in the snow along tree limb and scaffold,
lining rushes, capping cattails and teasel.

WHAT WINTER GRACES

In time, in season, tall reeds and grasses
etched by snow, and dazzling,
shall fall, to be replaced by others

and the arch, the canopy of snow-gilded branches, the canopy of
snow moss on thin black struts burning and blinding in the
morning sun shall fall, too, of its own accord, following the grasses
but slowly as if turnings and orbits meant less to steel

and the frame of latticed steel so firm overhead, though its deck
fall, bearing its ridges of ice and snow. Left to its own devices this
frame one day will fold upon itself into the steady river, into waters
babbling so nearly silent in winter, roaring and rumbling in spring.

More likely, long before rust and weather have had their way,
it will be cut apart with torches,
cut for scrap and hauled off, cut away as a hazard

as it has been a hazard, though closed, a quiet danger for those few
who venture here, who come as I do, not for travel, not for gaining
the other bank, but to watch and listen to the black rushing
current, to contemplate its defiant place in the air, to weep at its
blinding snow, to wonder how God so casually and deliberately,
with such prodigious and exacting care, graces the homely, the
feeble, the disrepaired.

I wonder that I have no answer,
only this fragile comfort—unsettling, inchoate—
that neither wood nor steel, nor limb nor rot nor rust, nor
   troubling water
shall obscure the joy that is here for the taking

nor span the currents of the broken heart.

GALLERY THREE:
Permanent Collection

❋

*I looked seaward, forced myself back
out into the bracing wind.
There at the end of a crude jetty made of rocks
a hooded man was staring into the monotony.
You don't speak to a man like that.
You give him all the room he needs.*

Stephen Dunn, "Backwaters," from *Different Hours*

*Then briefly as to yourselves:
Walk behind—as they do in France,
seventh class, or if you ride
Hell take curtains! Go with some show
of inconvenience: sit openly —
to the weather as to grief.
Or do you think you can shut grief in?*

William Carlos Williams, "Tract," from *Early Poems*

THIS MOST OBVIOUS OF THINGS

I am looking, as I leave, for a way
to say I love you, this most obvious of things.

It is mid-October, and I drive through valleys
alone, beneath blue sky both bright and unbroken

driving distractedly, despite my intentions,
slowed every mile by hillside after hillside

of brilliant red leaves, of vivid orange
leaves of shimmering gold against evergreen

as if the unplanned patterns lay like sky
unbroken, the impression of seamless difference

tugging the eyes like water eddying over stones
tugs the ear, thrilling the heart

until breathing is labored and hours
have passed without notice, slipping, gone.

Soon it will be dusk, then dark,
the texture of hillsides gone in darkness

the fabric, the folds of color gone black
as my destination draws nearer.

For a moment the straight western sun, burning
in the treetops, strikes west-facing slopes opposite

setting reds aflame, burnishing gold
until it nearly blinds, warming orange and brown

this whole world filled, unspeakably, with fire.
And I, unsentimental man that I am,

I, who have been looking for a way
who have wanted words for love, for you

who have felt now, my heart opened
and opening, who would bring you here with me

I, who would say *this is what love
must mean*, who would say foolish things

find myself doubly at a loss,
having seen heaven, alone.

BOTTLE

I have begun
the sober period
of my life.

One might think it
a kind of emptiness
a loss of particular joy.

Or, one might notice
how light catches skin
how light shatters

on the old air within
how it throws itself
across the wall.

For a moment
my long elegance
is shadowed within

the dancing light.
For a moment
I am free

of shape
I am free
of weight

I am free
of bottleness, of glass,
for a moment

the shadows
hold no memory
of hands.

MY FIRST HUSBAND

It is not something he would have wanted
years ago—this quiet, now frail fellow

carefully negotiating the steps down to his car.
He would never have allowed me to carry his bags.

And my mother, seventy-six, who follows,
all smiles and new clothes, who flows and bubbles,

pauses to marvel over my lilies with their red throats
just now in full bloom, just now reopened

to morning sun—my mother calling us back
here, where the lilies profuse, where light

and color converge; *here, now, a picture.*
Then, bags stowed, in the warble

of good-byes, offhandedly, she laughs
My first husband would never *have left this late,*

rejoicing in this new indulgence, perhaps
recalling a husband twenty years younger.

I smile for my mother, a bride again
after the long solitude of widowhood.

She deserves this happiness, this late flowering,
the secret intimacies of wanting what you have

and of being wanted. My wife and son wave
as the car turns carefully from the drive

tires grinding steadily on the gravel.
We wave toward windows gone blank in the sun.

These things converge in that instant:
the gritty sound of gravel, the empty windows,

the casual reference to her first husband—
the new finality of my father's death.

SAYING GOODBYE

Now that it is time to leave,

you gather all the family
you can manage into the car.

Leaving, you discover,
is an ailment all its own.

Nothing could have prepared you.

There is no natural language to say this.

Your hands flutter at car windows
toward windows where they,

Mom in one, Dad in another, hold back
curtains, faces shadowed,

untouched by morning sun,
diminishing figures reclaimed,

at a turn, by the land itself.
When they are lost from sight,

the car fills with silence,

a kind of grief, unspeakably personal,
welling from the heart's deep recess,

far deeper than any words formed
in memoriam.

ELEGY FOR MANY VOICES

Let us talk of eternity in this moment
Let us talk of frailty in this man

It is early afternoon in mid-November in New York.
As I drive south on the interstate,
a friend flies to his childhood home, hoping
to be known in his father's last hours.
Let us talk of eternity in these moments.

The trees on the hillsides are naked.
Needles of tamarack growing in clumps,
yellow now, appear like patches of sunlight.
In one leafless, smooth-barked sycamore
a red-tailed hawk watches the brown grass.
Let us talk of frailty in this man.

I am minutely aware of how motion and its absence
have fused. We wait, having waited.

A white mare gallops north across her pasture.
A truck flashing in steeply slanted sunlight
labors, soundlessly, up a distant hill.
I am aware of motion and cessation.
I know of silence, of its loss, the ubiquity of grief.
Let us talk of eternity in these moments.

As we go, having acquired, we divest:
a house, an apartment, now a room, a bed.
A life of giving, work, companionship

lets go, the hands working alone, gone idle.
Life and loss fusing. Having waited, we wait.
Let us talk of frailty in this man.

I know many things but I don't know enough.
While the family gathers—death pending—
I am traveling south on the interstate.
It is mid-November—in New York.
Having waited, we wait.
Let us talk of eternity in this moment.

A friend has flown to bury his father.
Oh, to know as one is known.
Now the sun lies far to the west,
tipping shadows from the trees, spilling
a darkness only sun reveals.
Let us talk of frailty in men.

*Let us talk of eternity, of human frailty, knowing
how motion subsides. The hawk circles, drops.
Having waited, we continue on.*

WORDS FOR HIS WIDOW

Now the house
is empty—
friends gone back
to other places;
family, children,
resuming their lives.

Quiet settles
like dust.

Today, the house
must be cleaned
—a tidy gesture
after the chaos
of condolences.

And tomorrow?

Tomorrow, perhaps,
pausing as you
climb the stairs,
touching
my picture
as you go,

you will sense how long
I have been away
— how young
I am becoming

—how we were happy.

Take that happiness with you
as you finish
climbing,

feeling too small
to fill this house,
every sound your own.

Would you have lived differently
had you known?
Would I?
Would it have made
this moment easier?

On the landing
you open the window
to unsettle the quiet.

The wild voices of water
rush in.

It is spring.
Last night's untimely snow
is melting,
running from the roof
running from the roofs
of all the houses
along the street.
Laughing, singing
it runs down
hill—water,
water everywhere

running
for the sea.
The river has blundered
over its banks,

churning, shouting!
you know the sound—

the furious insensible
loud river of grief.

CURRENCY

For fifteen years after we bought the house
we pried open windows frozen in decades of paint.

One by one, we worked with a putty knife,
chiseling its square blade between sash and frame,

breaking somehow the hideous layers of old paint.
Green. Gold. The vivid purple of iris and new bruises.

That first year we opened many to let the air in
to blow out decades of darkness, routine, privation,

took down the heavy draperies that dulled and muted daylight
painted the walls yellow and off-white and powder blue

to give the new light currency,
to keep it alive.

PILGRIM

It has been years since I entered the elevator
and rode its tiny room in the direction of heaven.

I can hear it clank and murmur still, coming
from that long vertical shaft that sends us up like prayers.

It is only human to let machines do what a body might—
even to wait on it to save some small effort.

I take to the stairs instead, its shaft a ziggurat
by which I climb, incrementally, closer and closer to God,

up and up, one grey tread at a time, each grey landing
like itself and all others, the handrail a ribbon, blood red.

No virtue attends my decision to climb as I
watch the young stand near the sliding door

waiting transport, except as muscle and blood embody faith.
Were this prayer, though it is not, I would bear it myself.

THE CLASSROOM

You will remember this: silence descending with dusk,
        your room ticking like a hot engine.
Faces that enlivened your youth, your morning,
        have worn you out, have gone.

You will remember this: once live bodies are gone
        heat lingers, heavy with sweat, burdened
            with musk. The air vibrates—chalk-
                board grey from erasures—
the ghost of SAVE THIS still legible
        in the top left corner.

You hear, somewhere down the hall,
        the distant wail of a vacuum.
You hear it rolling up and back, up and back,
        as the overhead lights, mirrored now
            in the wall of windows,
eclipse the last, lingering streaks of dusk—
        day plunged too soon into darkness.

In October, though daylight is reassigned
        to brighten your morning trek,
you arrive too early for sunrise and depart
        long past sunset. You cannot command daylight
            with a prod, a tap on the shoulder,
                its drooping eyes beyond your steely
glare.

You must face this just as
you must face the walk to your car,
       kicking through leaves that may have dazzled you
          at mid-day, a week ago, or two
                   that—fallen—blend
        into one shuffling slippered sibilant
            just as, shhhhhhhh,
you must face, later, the late labors, the reading,
      hoping for a tremor beneath boredom,
a hand reaching through the clutter
          toward yours.

THE OLD FEARS

All winter the car sat in a lot beside the road
as if to taunt me, rust appearing like new growth
across the crushed roof, in patterns on the scoured hood,
windshield pebbled on the dash, side windows shattered.

Through spring and far into summer the car sat
where, passing, I could see it front and back,
the front end sinking as its tires slowly exhaled
and I would always catch my breath, pull my eyes away.

A mile up that road, years later, as these things happen,
I hit my first deer. It raced from the undergrowth,
booming against fender and hood, scaling as if weightless
across the blacktop into the dry, weed-choked ditch.

So fast, as everyone notes, it happens so fast, like magic,
that the deer can't begin to bleed until it stops dead,
my foot just beginning to ease from the throttle
unformed cries escaping from somewhere deep in my chest.

Hands shaking, heart racing, breath rasping,
I walk the roadside 'til I find it in the weeds.
It might have been sleeping to my stunned eyes,
so small, so whole, so delicate. So perfectly formed.

Then, as if newly aware, I note the awkward bend of neck
and legs, the protruding tongue, the absolute stillness.
Longer, I stand, trying to take it in, hoping for— anything,
listening to gravel under my feet, to weeds growing, to my heart.

So I imagined every time I passed that broken car
the boom of collision, the airborne roll,
the roof landing, roof plowing through the dry cornfield
my boy hanging upside down by his seat harness.

Every passing, I am filled with the terror of those seconds
the imminent crash—the certain, crushing death.

Yet, as I see him find the buckle, roll out the window, unhurt,
I am crushed, again, by this mercy, I am broken.

GALLERY NOTES

Dedications

"Romance of Air and Bones" and "This Most Obvious of Things" written for Donna

"The Flood Sequence" written for Ian

"The Old Fears" written for Dylan

"Saying Goodbye" and "Elegy for Many Voices" written for J.F. Wardwell

Publications

"Pilgrim" was published in *Milieu*, Summer 2005

"Breaking the Ice," "The Interval," "Romance of Air and Bones," "This Most Obvious of Things," "Bottle," "Words for His Widow," "The Life of the River," and "New Snow" were published in *Stonework* Issue 2

"The Classroom" was accepted for publication in *The Tennessee English Journal*